READ THIS
BEFORE OUR NEXT MEETING

© 2011 Al Pittampalli

The Domino Project

Published by Do You Zoom, Inc.

The Domino Project is powered by Amazon. Sign up for updates and free stuff at www.thedominoproject.com.

This is the first edition. If you'd like to suggest a riff for a future edition, please visit our website.

Pittampalli, Al, 1983—

Read This Before Our Next Meeting: The modern meeting standard for successful organizations / Al Pittampalli

 p. cm.

ISBN 978-1-936719-16-7

Printed in the United States of America

READ THIS
BEFORE OUR NEXT MEETING

The modern meeting standard for successful organizations

By Al Pittampalli

THE
DOMINO
PROJECT
POWERED BY amazon.com

What Do You Do For A Living?

Someone asked me the other day what I do for a living. I found myself hard-pressed for an answer. If he wanted to know my job title, or what industry I worked in, then all I had to do was to recite what's on my business card. But he seemed sincere. He honestly wanted to know what I do most of the day, so I was honest, too: What I do for a living is attend meetings. Bad meetings.

I don't know how we've found ourselves in this place.

One mediocre meeting after another quietly corrodes our organization, and every day we allow it to happen. We've become so accustomed to long meetings, boring meetings, meetings lacking a clear purpose, that our curiosity about whether there might be a better alternative has faded into the background.

If we were to wake up for just a moment, we'd realize that two things are undeniable:

*   *   *

1. **We have too many meetings.**

2. **We have too many bad meetings.**

*   *   *

For years, we've been told by meeting experts that we have too many meetings. The experts remind us that if a memo suffices, we shouldn't have the meeting. But to no avail. Without hesitation, day after day, each one of us schedules meetings like the one we're about to attend today and, most certainly, tomorrow. A tragedy of the commons—everyone feels a benefit from calling a meeting, but few of us benefit from attending.

Over time, we've become nonchalant about bad meetings. If an operating room were as sloppily run as our meetings, patients would die. If a restaurant kitchen put as little planning into a meal as we put into our meetings, dinner would never be served.

But if that were the end of it, I wouldn't be writing this manifesto.

No, I'm sharing this with you, on the eve of our meeting because I've noticed something even more shocking than the colossal amount of time we're wasting at our organization. Worse than wasting time, the culture of useless meetings is changing us. It's becoming clear that our meeting culture is changing how we focus, what we focus on, and most important, what decisions we make

Yes. Meetings matter.

In simple organizations, not so much.
In industrial organizations, not so often.
In organizations that don't have to wrestle with change, not at all.

In our organization, though, and in modern organizations everywhere, meetings are the lever that allow coherent motion. Meetings are the way we make change, and change is how we grow.

We work in a business of complex problems. Meetings were the invention created to provide the needed coordination. We need meetings to ensure that intelligent decisions are made and to confirm that our teams are interacting effectively on complex projects.

What we don't need, though, are standard meetings, the mediocre meetings and the meetings that actually and actively cripple our organization.

Our meetings have evolved into something else entirely. We've fallen victim to mediocre meetings, not about coordination but about bureaucratic excuse making and the kabuki dance of company politics. We're now addicted to meetings that insulate us from the work we ought to be doing.

But this new way of thinking is not about blame; it's about opportunity. By changing a single tactic, by isolating and destroying the mediocre meeting, we can revamp the way projects are organized, decisions are made, and work gets done. We can reinvent the meeting and get back to the essential work of creation and coordination if we choose.

But we have to choose it. It's up to us and only us.

What could we do in a world with fewer meetings?

In a world with fewer meetings, we'd have more time for our real work, the work we do that actually propels our organization forward. The work we do that makes a difference to our company, to the customers, or to our shareholders: the programming, designing, selling, writing—the art.

We might finally have time to do what's important, not just what's urgent: mentor a colleague, connect with people in our industry, or practice our presentation to the board.

We'd have more time in the day to spend innovating and initiating new projects, instead of drowning in old ones that never seem to die.

Most of all, in a world where mediocre meetings had disappeared, we'd be forced to make and defend difficult decisions. When these mediocre meetings go away, so does the ability to adopt the easy compromise.

It's to serve this vision that I'm writing this to you. Not just for me, but on behalf of all of us, the entire organization.

The status quo must go. Now.

I have a solution, a plan I'd like to propose, a new standard we have to live by. But first, let's talk about the two most serious dangers of our current meeting system.

*   *   *

1. **Traditional meetings create a culture of compromise.**

2. **Traditional meetings kill our sense of urgency.**

*   *   *

Traditional Meetings Create a Culture of Compromise

Writing this, I'm reminded of a Wall Street Journal article I read years ago about Brad Garlinghouse, senior VP at Yahoo!. Meeting culture was so debilitating at Yahoo! that he mustered the courage to send to top staff a memo that included this paragraph:

> I believe we must embrace our problems and challenges and that we must take decisive action. We have the opportunity—in fact the invitation—to send a strong, clear and powerful message to our shareholders and Wall Street, to our advertisers and our partners, to our employees (both current and future), and to our users. They are all begging for a signal that we recognize and understand our problems, and that we are charting a course for fundamental change. Our current course and speed simply will not get us there. Short-term band-aids will not get us there.

The truth of his memo was so clear and so shocking that someone leaked the memo to the press. The entire world was now watching to see what Yahoo! would do. But nothing decisive followed. No real action took place. They stagnated. During the birth of Web 2.0—the age of Google and Twitter and Facebook and Groupon—Yahoo!, the company that could have won, did nothing.

It wasn't because Yahoo! didn't have smart people. They did. It wasn't because Yahoo! didn't have access to capital or technology or the market. They had all three. The reason Yahoo! failed is simple:

By default, Yahoo! had adopted a culture of failed meetings. Those meetings killed action and, most of all, created a culture of compromise.

Sadly, our organization is slipping in that very same direction.

When's the last time any one of us made a game-changing decision that made our hearts race?

I can't recall. Can you?

Instead of a meeting structure that demands that we make and defend strong decisions, the broken meeting system we've adopted enables us to pass off responsibility too easily.

Our organization is in desperate need of innovative ideas, gutsy ones, the kinds that are essential in our new hyper-competitive marketplace. But we can't forget: ideas don't bring their own commitment or perseverance; only humans do that.

Change is never met with open arms. Great decisions involve risk and risk scares people; it's natural for great ideas to get attacked or, worse, ignored. I can think of no single great innovation that has ever happened without the presence of opposition.

In order for our idea to have a chance of surviving this initial inquisition, it has to have a champion. One individual willing to step up, take responsibility for it, grab on tight, and push in the face of that opposition.

But alas, our traditional meetings kill game-changing ideas. When a revolutionary idea is brought into our meetings (and many have been), no one takes ownership. The bystander effect takes over.

As if we were witnessing a petty crime on a street filled with other on-lookers, we feel little pressure to take action. After all, as we sit in our safe conference room, it's hard not to assume that the responsibility should be shared by everyone. The table is round, there's a sense of egalitarian fairness, and we assume that we're all in this together. But that diffusion of responsibility is what sabotages our hopes for innovation.

The committee adopts the decision, the idea gets watered down, the corners are cut off, and the result is a safe (or no) decision, creating little change and little hope for a better future.

At the British Broadcasting Company, significant purchases often require six or more meetings by different boards and review panels.

A top BBC executive writes:

> Some of this issue is organisational and comes from ambiguous responsibilities, while another part is the risk averse nature of individuals. In the BBC, I find that decisions tend not to be made independently, even though performance management is low key and individuals are less likely to be held accountable.

Like the BBC, we fear a ghost—the ghost of the decision made, the urgent move forward.

What are we so afraid of? If we make the wrong decision, so be it. Will we die? Probably not. We'll recover, stronger, but to make no decision is to guarantee our eventual demise.

Let's get out of the stands and on to the court.

Traditional Meetings Kill Our Sense of Urgency

Or as John Kotter says, our compulsive determination to move and win, now.

When did we lose our fire? When did we get so comfortable? I used to come into work with a promise to myself, a commitment to do work that matters. But having been unsuccessful in fulfilling that promise in the short windows between meetings, I now come into work with the hope of surviving the day.

I wonder when we'll realize what a trap we've set for ourselves. Regularly interrupting the day to bring our best minds together to focus on the urgent makes it impossible for these people to spend their focused energy on what's actually important. We have created a culture designed to survive the urgent by watering it down, instead of challenging our best to step up and lead us to do the important.

Peter Drucker tells us that meetings are by definition a concession to deficient organization. We either meet or work. We can't do both at the same time.

Real work is what moves us forward. Work that involves action, struggle, and effort. It's that output that puts us closer to winning. If the mission could speak, it would constantly tell us, "get back to work."

The most talented among us know that they best serve the organization by making things. We add value only by producing work that contributes directly toward our goals and by initiating amazing work that wasn't even asked of us. Instead, we're pulled into meetings.

David Heinemer Hansson, from 37 Signals, says meetings are toxic because they break workdays into a series of work moments. Achieving flow, the state in which we do our best work, can take long periods of focus. Interruptions force us to start over each time.

I'm tired of starting over.

Efficient systems should be organized around the output that wants to be optimized: in our case, the work. But with so many meetings called, it's as if our work is organized around our meetings instead.

Sometimes, when I'm called into a meeting, I wonder what could possibly be so urgent that it pulls me away from my real work. As with the yellow "BREAKING NEWS" banner that appears on CNN every time I turn it on, I'm skeptical. And after the meeting is over and I'm forced to confront the truth that no, there was no real urgency, I'm disappointed, angry. I feel betrayed.

This false urgency is echoed in three common meeting types:

1. Convenience meetings

2. Formality meetings

3. Social meetings

Convenience meetings:

Meetings called because it's difficult to capture everything we want to say effectively in writing, quickly. These meetings rarely add any more value than a memo would have. In fact, they're worse because in addition to wasting time, they rely on nonverbal communication that's hard to refer to later on.

Formality meetings:

Meetings called by managers who think it's their job to hold them. It doesn't matter whether these meetings are designed to give off the appearance of control and productivity, or whether they're a way for managers to subtly exert their status; in either case, these meetings are wasteful. Even if having convening members get together to share advice or status reports results in some incremental benefit, it pales in comparison to the cost of the interruption.

Social meetings:

Meetings for the purpose of connection. We sometimes call social meetings without even realizing it. I'm guilty of this myself. Unfortunately, social meetings quickly turn circular and expand to fit the time. You might want to slow down and chat, but perhaps not everyone in the room has the same goals (or time) that you do.

* * *

Once we're exposed to the callous indifference of a false-urgent meeting, we begin to question everything th`e organization does. If management is willing to regularly tolerate such an affront on our productivity, why bother?

Meetings need to be less like the endless commercial breaks during a football game, and more like pit stops at the Daytona 500. Sure, even these stops slow momentum, but not for long, and only in service of winning. Quick high-energy transactions to refuel, to change the tires, to allow the driver to do the work better and faster—that's the type of meeting that people will walk away from with a continued sense of urgency and energized with a feeling of aliveness.

Maybe even more unsettling than the false-urgency problem is that meetings have become a tool to delay decisions. They have become our default stalling tactic.

I fear we have become politicians.

I recently saw a town hall meeting on television, featuring a candidate for state senate. When confronted with questions from the audience that would force him to make tough decisions, he dodged, and instead scheduled future meetings. Not surprising for a politician desperately trying to hold on to votes.

But this scenario is eerily similar to ones I've seen in our organization.

Like all human beings, we're terrified of making decisions. In the face of pressing, difficult decisions, we stall. Meetings are a socially acceptable and readily available way of doing so.

This is why we find them so useful. Meetings provide a forum for us to gather more and more intelligence indefinitely, and the emotional assurance from surrounding ourselves with others alleviates the fear (at least temporarily).

We have to remember that we can never guarantee a good outcome, no matter how much planning we do. Thoughtfulness is important, but so is speed. A system that allows the use of meetings as a stalling tactic leads to a culture of indecisiveness that is no longer acceptable.

The system is broken. But it's not too late to fix it.

What's not a meeting?

In our traditional system, we've used the word "meeting" to describe almost every type of professional gathering. We won't do that anymore because words are important.

From now on, we'll use "meeting" to define only a precise type of session.

Before we do, let's talk about what's not a meeting.

1. Conversations

2. Group work sessions

3. Brainstorms

*   *   *

Conversations:

A conversation is a real-time dialogue between two people; it's not a meeting. Conversations are easy to control, easy to decline, and normally an effective form of communication. The conversation isn't too dangerous because:

1. We're generally good at conversations.

2. Unlike meetings, conversations are not weapons of mass interruption.

Group work sessions:

A group work session is exactly what it sounds like; it's not a meeting. It's real work done simultaneously with other team members, intra-team and often ad hoc. Example: Three of our writers get together and combine their talents to pump out copy that was more powerful than they could've written by themselves. The focus is creation, the purpose is clear, and the session includes only team members who interact with each other on a regular basis, anyway.

Brainstorms:

Brainstorms are magical sessions specifically designed for generating lots of ideas. These are special. So special that we'll revisit them a little bit later. But a brainstorm is not a meeting.

*   *   *

We're left with the Modern Meeting

Now we get to the answer. A new kind of meeting—the Modern Meeting Standard. Starting today, that's how we're going to do business.

Traditional meetings are treated as just another form of communication. Just another item to be included in the same category as e-mail, memos, and phone calls. That's an error in judgment.

Meetings are too expensive and disruptive to justify using them for the most common types of communication, like making announcements, clarifying issues, or even gathering intelligence.

Like war, meetings are a last resort.

The Modern Meeting is a special instrument, a sacred tool that exists for only one reason: to support decisions.

Decisions have always been what moves us to act. They precede all change. They define our organization.

Brave decisions lead to a brave organization; fearful decisions lead to a fearful one.

So the opportunity is this: we must structure the Modern Meeting so that bold decisions happen often and quickly, and those decisions are converted into movement that leads our organization forward—fearlessly. The Modern Meeting optimizes for the decision.

The Seven Principles of Modern Meetings

1. **The Modern Meeting**
   supports a decision that has
   already been made.

2. **The Modern Meeting**
   moves fast and ends on schedule.

3. **The Modern Meeting**
   limits the number of attendees.

4. **The Modern Meeting**
   rejects the unprepared.

5. **The Modern Meeting**
   produces committed action plans.

6. **The Modern Meeting**
   refuses to be informational.
   Reading memos is mandatory.

7. **The Modern Meeting**
   works only alongside a culture
   of brainstorming.

The Modern Meeting convenes to support a decision that has already been made.

Our organization is experiencing a decision deficit. We run into the constant trap of over-planning. We have a cycle of never-ending due diligence. We should gather only as much input and advice from others as is necessary to make our decision. After all, decisions are the job of the individual.

Before you make your preliminary decision, you aren't allowed to call a meeting. If you invite me to a Modern Meeting for which a clear decision hasn't been established, I'll look at you, puzzled. I might even walk out. Modern Meetings can't exist without a decision to support. Not a question to discuss—a decision.

This principle will stop the over-planning and mass interruption that occur so often. With one click of a button, the decision maker disrupts seven people's schedules for one hour, just to help make a decision. The Modern Meeting won't allow it.

If you need my input pre-decision, you'll have to get it from me personally. We'll have a conversation. Less convenient for you, but that's the point. You're the one with the looming decision to make, not me.

Only after you make a preliminary decision can a meeting be called with the relevant stakeholders to arrive at a final resolution.

If the decision is controversial, get buy-in from the group (via one-on-one conversations) before you make your decision. If we still have serious objections or better alternatives, or we want to propose changes to the details of the decision, the Modern Meeting is the forum for debating them. In the end, though, you make the decision; you own the outcome.

The Modern Meeting has a bias for action.
To insulate ourselves from potential failure and "wrong" maneuvers, our organization has leaned for years toward prudence.

The Modern Meeting leans toward speed.

Sure, some decisions will fail. But movement even occasionally in the wrong direction is far better than standing still.

The benefits that quick decisions bring are boundless. Sometimes it just takes the conviction, the competence, and the guts to make them.

The Modern Meeting focuses on the only two activities worth convening for: conflict and coordination.

Conflict:
The individual should own her decisions and champion them strongly, but in our organization we must be open to input from others. We should be resolute, without being stubborn.

Conflicting opinions spur debate that can open the door to intelligent decisions. The Modern Meeting welcomes conflict. After a preliminary decision is made, if there are differing opinions or serious objections, the Modern Meeting gets them all out on the table to be considered.

In traditional meetings, individuals may hesitate to voice their true opinions or edgy ideas for fear of criticism. They may think: Is it the right time to dissent?

The Modern Meeting meets only for the purpose of dissent. Conflict is expected, so participants feel safe to let their ideas fly indiscriminately.

One caveat: Upon making a decision, if you're not willing to alter it or modify it in any way, don't bother having a Modern Meeting. Just go.

Conflict is useless unless you, the decision maker, come to the table with an open mind. That doesn't mean that you shouldn't be confident in your decision, nor should you easily compromise, but you should be moveable. Otherwise, don't call a meeting. Make the decision, send a memo, and be done with it.

Coordination:
Decisions can lead to profound action, but that action happens only with proper coordination.

Once a decision is reached, sometimes the resulting action is straightforward. The division of labor is clear; the intersections between teams and departments are obvious. No need to have a meeting.

Other times, the scenarios are tricky, the steps are vague. It's worth having a Modern Meeting to engage in collaborative problem solving. Getting smart people in a room to figure out how to support a plan or launch a product makes sense.

The Modern Meeting moves fast and ends on schedule.

Traditional meetings seem to go on forever, with no end in sight. When the clock runs out, we add more time or, even worse, more meetings.

Deadlines are procrastination's worst enemy.

Just a couple of months ago, at the eleventh hour, the House, the Senate, and the Obama administration finally came to an agreement on a budget for the upcoming fiscal year, moments before a deadline that would have led to a massive government shutdown. Coincidence?

Strong deadlines force parties to resolve the hard decisions necessary for progress.

Let's contrast our meetings with those of the senior executives at Ritz-Carlton in Atlanta. They gather in the hallway of the president's office for a talk that lasts under ten minutes. No chitchat, no sitting, just high-energy business. The instigator gets buy-in, a decision is resolved, and they move on.

With too much time, even the most unshakable decision will be reconsidered. Arguments turn circular; the same points occur over and over again without more real information being added to the debate. More time leads to more doubt. More doubt leads to more anxiety. More anxiety makes the decision fall apart.

Keep meetings as brief as possible and set a firm end time. Every minute that you are sitting with five or seven of our key people is a minute that's costing us a fortune. Spend it wisely.

The Modern Meeting limits the number of attendees.

We invite too many people to our meetings. You don't want to offend people and neither do I. I've been guilty of being both the offender and the offended. So have you.

We can't worry about hurting people's feelings anymore, because we do so at the sacrifice of the decision while wasting valuable time in the process.

When we try to reach an agreement in our meetings, the number of actual agreements that need to take place rises exponentially as more people are added to the group.

With two people, you need one agreement for unanimity. With four people, you need six agreements. With a group of ten, forty-five agreements must be made to come to a consensus on anything.

Adding more department heads and more bystanders seems like a good idea, but when there are too many conflicting views, there's rarely any basis for agreement. Worse, having people merely watch wastes their time and diminishes their stature.

In the Modern Meeting, we invite only the people who are absolutely necessary for resolving the decision that has been presented.

Every member of any meeting should ask himself these questions:

- Will you be able to function if you read about the meeting after it's over?

- If you are given the decision we're discussing in advance, can you give me your opinion in advance?

- Do you add any value by sitting in the meeting without participating?

- Are you attending symbolically, or simply as a way to demonstrate your power?

If you have no strong opinion, have no interest in the outcome, and are not instrumental for any coordination that needs to take place, we don't need you. From now on, if you're invited to a meeting where you don't belong, please don't attend.

The Modern Meeting rejects the unprepared.

Traditional meetings were communication tools, often beginning with the dissemination of information. Preparation seemed at best redundant, at worst a waste of time.

Not in the Modern Meeting.

Preparation starts with the meeting leader. He must create an agenda and a set of background materials.

An agenda is a map, a symbol, a driver's license. It shows people that this is a Modern Meeting and that you're serious about driving. If you want to earn my eager participation, spend the time to create an agenda. A useful agenda requires thought and hard choices—it's not just a few bullet points.

Preparing an agenda involves thinking through what's going to happen at the meeting—what the objectives are, who should be invited, what they should bring, and how long the meeting will last.

Second, agendas establish the decision that is being discussed and elicits feedback and suggestions.

The agenda should clearly state the problem, the alternatives, and the decision. It should outline exactly the sort of feedback requested, and it should end with a statement of what this meeting will deliver if it's successful. Anything that's not on the agenda doesn't belong in the meeting.

Third (and most important), agendas demand preparation on the part of the attendees.

Every meeting should require pre-meeting work. Any information for getting attendees up to speed should be given out beforehand. If the attendee doesn't have time to read and prepare, she doesn't have time to attend.

The Modern Meeting is about conflict and coordination, two activities that hinge upon preparation.

After all, how can you thoughtfully debate a decision, or intelligently coordinate its resulting action, upon having heard it for the first time?

The Modern Meeting demands that you carefully think through all the different scenarios presented by the decision and come up with thoughtful responses.

In our purposeless traditional meeting, your impromptu comments once sounded intelligent; in the Modern Meeting, they'll sound unsubstantial.

If someone comes unprepared, cancel the meeting or hold it without him. In exchange for your preparation, we promise you an intense, very short meeting where something actually gets done.

If someone comes and doesn't participate, don't invite her to the next meeting.

This is not high school; we strive to be a world-class organization. We can't tolerate your unpreparedness anymore. Unprepared participants are dead weight.

Sometimes the worst offenders are our top executives. They stroll into the meeting room, empty-handed, waiting to be briefed as if they were King. But they're not.

In the Modern Meeting, the decision is King. All hail the King.

The Modern Meeting produces committed action plans.

In traditional meetings, minutes were recorded. Because meetings lacked a clear purpose, it was the only way for us to record what happened in them.

In the Modern Meeting, minutes are not required. We don't need to know the details of what happened at the meeting, because it's the same thing that happens at every Modern Meeting: conflict and coordination. All we need to know is the decision and the resulting action plan.

If you don't receive an action plan from the meeting I invited you to attend, you have every right not to attend my next one.

Part of the obligation of the Modern Meeting is that if you want attendance, you must reciprocate with an action plan. That plan should include at least the following:

- What actions are we committing to?

- Who is responsible for each action?

- When will those actions be completed?

A scribe should record and restate the action items to the group to gain agreement that they haven't been misinterpreted. If we're not clear, it impedes the very coordination that the meeting was called to create.

After the meeting, the leader should make sure participants are doing what they agreed to do, when they agreed to do it. Hold them accountable. If you don't, who will?

Let's put pressure on the action owners to complete their tasks and pull the meeting full circle. The Modern Meeting is compulsively concerned with justifying its existence. Completed action plans show the meeting participants that the time they spent in the conference room wasn't in vain. The meeting worked.

The Modern Meeting refuses to be informational. Reading memos is mandatory.

In our organization, we've learned that the only way to ensure that our message is heard is to hold a meeting.

I know this from experience. All too often, I send out important e-mail messages, only to have them be read by just a few people.

The Modern Meeting cannot survive in an organization that fails to read.

We must keep meetings about decisions. They must stay sacred. The only way to do so is to cancel the informational meetings.

Of course, we'll all have to agree on a pact: we'll cancel the informational meetings, but you must commit to reading the memos.

We all have to treat this agreement very seriously. If we don't read the memo, the pact is broken, and the informational meeting is inevitable. It takes only a few individuals to falter for the entire system of trust to crumble.

In fairness, I don't always communicate in a way that is effective. The Modern Meeting requires that you don't dribble your thoughts in an endless series of instant messages and e-mails. No, you have to share your thoughts in coherent, cogent documents. These must be complete thoughts that are actually worth reading and responding to. And indicate true priority. Signal to the rest of us when something requires extra attention, without crying wolf too often.

.

The Modern Meeting works only alongside a culture of brainstorming.

Putting brainstorms alongside the Modern Meeting method may seem like a non sequitur, but the brainstorm is so crucial to the success of the Modern Meeting, it justly fits here.

The brainstorm is the anti-meeting, the counterweight that sits on the other end of the scale, opposite the Modern Meeting, giving the system balance.

After all, the Modern Meeting is focused around decision, which in its Latin root, decir, means to kill off possibilities. It's the medicine we need to move forward.

But we also need sessions dedicated to the creation of possibilities. A place where the imagination is allowed to roam free and generate a plethora of ideas, from which innovation can be born.

The goal of brainstorming is to break free from the fear that often restricts people's creativity.

Experts agree that the best way to get great results is to make brainstorming fun, to create a moment that lacks evaluation and criticism. It's this difference in setting, mood, and rules that signals to the group: it's safe to take risks here. And most of all, bring in people with nothing to lose.

I believe that just about anyone is capable of participating productively in a brainstorming session, but with one important caveat: the closer the topic is to the work you do all day, the worse you will perform.

This means that the internal dialogue about avoiding risk is particularly lousy when you ask responsible parties to brainstorm. After all, they're the ones who will be held responsible for executing what they just dreamed up.

In every brainstorming session I've attended, the untrained participants are easily identified. They start to speak up, then realize that they might have to live with what they propose or that they might be criticized, and hey, it's easier to just listen.

We should look to firms like IDEO, one of the most creative and innovative in the world. They believe brainstorming is a very different type of activity from what usually takes place inside conference rooms. If you're going to brainstorm, that's all you should do. Innovation is sacred.

The ground rules:

1. Let's invite people who are passionate about the idea. A passionate intern is better than a disinterested executive.

2. Let's praise liberally. No criticism, not even evaluation. This is not a regular meeting. If it turns into one, then we have failed. Let's make sure that the measured output of the meeting is the breadth and quantity of ideas.

3. Let's number our ideas. IDEO head Tom Kelly recommends deciding how many ideas you want to have and then shooting for that number. This method forces people to let go of their filters in service of meeting the target number of ideas.

4. Let's use a timer. It's toward the very end that people start flinging up last-minute ideas to meet the mark. Perversely, tension helps us overcome fear.

5. Let's have fun. (Most of us have forgotten how to have fun at work.)

6. Let's get active. Encourage people to stand up, walk around the room. In fact, get out of the room. Brainstorming always works better in a place reserved for just that. If the room is the very same place where you got excoriated for a lousy quarter, it's hard to feel confident.

7. Let's have a clear focus. Make sure the brainstorm is free, but not a free-for-all. The ideas should be targeted in the direction of the problem at hand. Create a clear problem statement and make sure people are on task.

8. Let's have a strong facilitator (or an expert). The cost of even the best brainstorming expert is tiny compared to the benefit you'll get and the time you'll save. In addition, an external voice can change the tone in the room more easily than you can.

9. Let's not invite the boss or the VP of No into the room. You have to make the environment feel safe for people to suggest ideas that are risky, even controversial. If there is a key leader who is clearly holding the session back, that person needs to go.

10. Let's write it all down. A non-participant should chronicle everything, even the silly stuff.

* * *

You Must Decide

There is a large gap between where our organization is and where it needs to be. It's not a crevice, but it's not a canyon, either.

I'm convinced that this gap is our meetings.

The solution comes down to choice. We attend meetings led by our boss, our colleagues, consultants, and even our clients because we don't feel we have any other choice. Much like a witness being subpoenaed to testify in court, our presence is mandatory.

But if you ask the people running these meetings, they'll tell you that they feel as if they have no choice, either. They don't feel in control; the system is in control. The meeting, it turns out, is a get-together of the passive, called by someone who feels as if he has no choice.

You do have a choice. So do I.

We might not be able to control all the meetings we attend, but right now, we can take a step toward controlling the way the system encourages and defines meetings.

In the long run, the Modern Meeting lasts only if everyone agrees to adopt it. It's an all-or-nothing proposition.

But in the short run, as with installing an upgrade of Microsoft Word, if we live the standard, those around us will have no choice but to join us.

No more can we pretend that the system is not wrong. It is.

No more will we allow our time to be consistently wasted thirty minutes at a time. Our time is too precious, too fleeting.

No more will we succumb to meetings that are ineffective or incompetent. We are too effective, too competent.

We must demand a culture where bad meetings aren't tolerated. If you hold a meeting that wastes the time of your colleagues, you're blacklisted. We need a culture where people don't dare show up to a meeting late or, even worse, unprepared, for fear of being shunned. We deserve a culture where the strong spirit of teamwork brings out the best of the group, not the worst of the individual.

Culture change occurs when a transformational idea spreads to enough people that a massive paradigm shift occurs.

Like a virus that makes its way from person to person, spreading exponentially faster, so can the Modern Meeting, until so many people adopt it that a new meeting culture emerges.

I beg you to share the ideas in this manifesto with everyone in your organization who has eyes to read it. Share it as if the organization depends on it. Because it does.

I love this organization. I love it too much to hold back the truth, even at the risk of offending others.

Therefore, I won't be attending our upcoming meeting. It's my first, but certainly not last, action in allegiance to the Modern Meeting.

Iacta alea esto. The die is cast.

I don't mean this in the grave way that Julius Caesar did when he crossed the Rubicon to begin a civil war in the Roman Empire.

I say this to you in a frenzy of excitement, of great opportunity. The way it was meant when it was originally written by Menander, the ancient Greek dramatist:

> *Let the game be ventured.*

The Modern Meeting Standard

We are tired of wasting time.

Meetings are a mess; here is how we will fix them:

The Modern Meeting supports a decision that has already been made.

If a decision maker needs advice pre-decision, he should get it from others in one-on-one conversations. Only after a preliminary decision is made can a meeting be convened.

A meeting might be necessary for either of two reasons:

Conflict:

The relevant stakeholders can debate the decision, propose alternatives, suggest modifications, or have concerns addressed. The decision is ultimately resolved.

Coordination:

If a decision demands complex collaboration from different teams or departments, stakeholders can convene to coordinate an action plan.

The Modern Meeting starts on time, moves fast, and ends on schedule.

The Modern Meeting enforces firm meeting end times to ensure that the decisions aren't delayed needlessly. The meeting ends, a decision is resolved and participants get back to work.

If you are late, we will start without you. And we won't invite you next time.

The Modern Meeting limits the number of attendees.

Only people who are critical to the outcome are invited to a Modern Meeting. Small numbers allow decisions to be resolved quickly and plans to be coordinated smoothly. If invited attendees recognize that they don't need to be there, it's their obligation to decline.

The Modern Meeting rejects the unprepared.

An agenda is distributed well in advance of a Modern Meeting, and it establishes the decision being debated or the action being coordinated. The Modern Meeting demands that you carefully think through all the different scenarios presented by the decision and come up with thoughtful responses. We will call on you. If you are not prepared, do not attend.

The Modern Meeting produces committed action plans.

What actions are we committing to? Who is responsible for each action? When will those actions be completed? The Modern Meeting ensures that these questions are answered and distributes the resulting action plan soon after the meeting ends. It's the meeting leader's responsibility to follow up and hold participants accountable for their commitments.

If no action plan is necessary, neither is a meeting.

The Modern Meeting refuses to be informational. Reading memos is mandatory.

In order to keep modern meetings strictly in support of decisions, informational meetings are cancelled. For this to be possible, managers will write memos instead, but everyone must commit to reading them. In a culture of reading, informational meetings are no longer necessary.

The Modern Meeting works only alongside a culture of brainstorming.

The Modern Meeting is about decision, the narrowing of options. Brainstorming is the necessary complement, as it results in the mass generation of options. Brainstorming has to be done correctly, though. It's an anti-meeting, so the regular rules of the Modern Meeting don't apply.

Frequently Asked Questions about the Modern Meeting

What is the essence of the Modern Meeting?

The Modern Meeting is above all an attitude, a posture that looks at meetings as a sacred tool for forward momentum, instead of a retarding force working against change. The Modern Meeting is dedicated to eliminating waste and creating a culture of decisive action.

How do I get upper management to embrace the Modern Meeting?

You won't. Not at first. That's fine.

Do your meetings your way. Persuade just one boss, one supervisor, one manager to adopt the Modern Meeting.

Sometimes senior leadership is the last to change. Focus on sharing the Modern Meeting with your direct colleagues, team, and department first. Then share it with other departments inside the organization.

Are daily status meetings Modern Meetings?

No. Regularly scheduled status meetings are a hybrid of social, formality, and convenience meetings. They're usually less about decision making and more about habit. There are many efficient technology tools, like BaseCamp, that you can use for status reporting instead.

Try a month without status meetings and see what happens. My guess is, you won't miss them as much as you think.

How can a leader communicate bad or sensitive news to a large group of people without a traditional meeting?

Try this instead: Have the leader record and send out a video memo— it's a start, something people can watch in private.

The follow-up is essential: hold office hours. Encourage people who have questions and concerns to schedule one-on-one conversations with the leader or others who can actually do something about the situation.

People want respect. They don't want a crowded room filled with frightened people and no chance to speak up.

What are some organizations that do meetings well?

Amazon, Google, and Intel are all notable in their meeting practices and share many of the elements of the Modern Meeting.

So are you telling me that when I have a decision to make, the first step is to reach out to people individually for advice?

Actually, the very first step is deciding how to decide.

Ask yourself:

Can I make this decision myself?

If a group is necessary, how and when should I involve this group?

Should this decision be made intuitively or analytically?

Does the opinion of someone else matter? Or are facts sufficient?

Can I do this with a conversation instead of a meeting?

How much time should this decision take?

What should my next step be?

Are you serious about using a timer for meetings?

Dead serious. Buy the Kikkerland tape timer for each conference room, or buy the TIM (Time Is Money) digital timer if you want to get fancy. Best investment you'll ever make under $25.

A visual reminder that the clock is ticking keeps meetings on schedule and shows participants you mean business.

Will instituting the Modern Meeting reduce our total number of meetings?

Drastically, yes. If it doesn't, you're doing something wrong. One of the key tenets of the Modern Meeting is that they're scarce, and thus more valuable than traditional meetings.

How often should we brainstorm?

Brainstorming, done right, generates a huge surplus of innovation, more than your organization can handle. As with filling up the gas tank, you need to stop pumping before you waste ideas.

A culture of brainstorming is a culture of urgency. It's a recognition that there are infinite opportunities that can be capitalized on if we can recognize them and move on them now.

Once you get competent at brainstorming, you'll discover that your organization will hustle to keep up, creating a need for ever more innovation.

Of course, this isn't a book about brainstorming. If you're not trained, go find some great books or take a course. The books by Michael Michalko are a great place to start.

What do we do if more than one person has authority over a decision?

Force one person to step up and own the decision.

"Hey, Mike and Ashwin, I want to establish myself as the owner of this decision. I'd like to include your input on the decision, but since the Modern Meeting requires only one owner, I'd like to take the primary responsibility for making this decision."

Don't wait for the other person to step up. When in doubt, own the decision yourself.

Aren't impromptu meetings necessary sometimes? What if it's an emergency?

Not only is holding an ad hoc meeting a massive interruption for those around you, but it's usually not effective for sound decision making.

If immediacy is an issue, consult one or two advisors, and then make the decision by yourself.

But remember, it's almost always a better idea to spend a second deciding how to decide first. How much time do I really have to make this decision? What are the ramifications of this decision? Whom do I absolutely need to consult with to make the best decision?

Should I structure the meeting time into sections?

The leader should dictate the meeting flow instead of blindly following a predetermined timing structure.

The Modern Meeting centers around conflict and coordination, two activities that are often difficult to fit into tiny timeslots. Although some structure can help the meeting run efficiently (especially with larger meetings), too much structure can choke the spontaneity of comment and thought that leads to constructive debate and great solutions.

How should I deal with diversions as they arise in our meeting?

Ruthlessly. As leader, don't let diversions distract the group from the core purpose of the meeting. We don't have any time for grandstanding, blame, or verbal wandering. It's your job to politely shut down those who veer off course.

How do I open the meeting?

Meeting time is a precious resource too valuable to be squandered. No need to bring people up to speed or have people go around the room and introduce themselves. Engage people by briefly visiting what's at stake, and then move right into the heart of the matter.

What's the posture I should take as I run the meeting?

Benevolent dictatorship. The outcome rests on your shoulders, so make the meeting work. Be confident, strong, and flexible. Don't make apologies for taking the meeting in any direction you see fit to reach the final destination.

Does every decision require a meeting?

Some decisions are unilateral, are non-controversial, and require little coordination. Just notify the affected parties and you're done. No meeting necessary.

Other decisions are more critical, are controversial, and/or require collaborative problem solving for their implementation. Go ahead and hold a meeting.

Does it make sense for conflict and coordination to occur at the same meeting?

When you're convening a Modern Meeting, it's important that you're clear about the state of your decision. Are you resolute in your decision? Then inform participants that the purpose of the meeting is merely to debate details of that decision or to address concerns about the ramifications. In this case, one meeting can serve to finalize the decision and coordinate a full action plan.

Are there any exceptions?

Modern Meetings can lead to major insights that cause a reevaluation of the initial decision (this is the point of group conflict). Occasionally, it's wise for the decision maker to take a little more time to consider these new points of view, hold additional follow-up conversations with certain participants, or retrieve a bit more information to make a decision.

Careful, though. If this practice turns into a frequently used stalling tactic, it jeopardizes the entire system. By the end of the meeting, the decision maker at least needs to set a firm decision date (an uncomfortably imminent deadline, preferably within forty-eight hours).

Do I always have to make a decision by myself?

Group decision making often leads to a culture of compromise. However, there are times when it may be appropriate for you to outsource to the group (for example, by holding a vote). Still, it's your decision, your process, and you're fully responsible for the outcome.

As a meeting participant, what should I consider as I prepare?

A few questions to ask yourself: What is my position on this decision? How can I intelligently and persuasively present that position? Are there data or stories that I can use? What role will I need to play in the coordination of this decision? What do I need from other members in order to fulfill my part of the action plan?

If everyone is in agreement on a decision, does that mean that no meeting should be held?

Premature harmony can be dangerous for critical decisions. You can use a Modern Meeting to foster conflict that hasn't occurred yet.

Do all participants need to stay for the entire meeting?

Of course not. If their presence is no longer required, send them home.

How far in advance should I schedule a meeting?

Not providing enough time contributes to a culture of false urgency. Ask yourself two questions:

Are you giving people enough advance warning to respect their schedules and priorities?

Are you scheduling meetings soon enough so that momentum builds instead of wanes?

How do I initiate a meeting?

Have you first determined that your meeting is necessary?

OK, make a list of the people you want to invite. Then cross off everyone except those members who are absolutely critical to the meeting's purpose. It's not about sparing feelings, it's about moving forward.

Create a detailed agenda and then ask yourself one more time: Is this meeting really necessary? If so, send out personal invites to participants. Once they know it's a Modern Meeting, they'll come, and they'll come prepared.

What's the most important thing to remember when inviting someone to a meeting?

It's a sales pitch. You're not selling them your decision; you're selling them on the process, a new and better way to move forward.

Tell them, with enthusiasm, what's at stake. Explain to them specifically why they're being invited. Persuade them as if they have the right and the obligation to decline weak invitations, because they do.

Can you show me a sample agenda?

You can find one at: ModernMeetingStandard.com.

What if I end up making a decision that not everyone agrees with?

Congratulations are in order. You're a leader.

How do I decline a meeting that I won't add value to?

Politely but directly: "Hi, Keyvon—After reviewing your meeting agenda, I've decided that although this decision affects my team, I have no strong opinion on the matter, nor do I feel uniquely qualified to participate. Please send me the meeting summary, and I'll be happy to contribute to the implementation of this decision."

Can we spread Modern Meetings to groups outside our organization, like our vendors and our clients?

You must. The best way to ensure that your meetings with other organizations are Modern is to help spread the idea.

Teach your vendors and clients the Modern Meeting method, share the vision with them, and encourage them to adopt it for their own organizations. If it spreads, we all win.

This is how e-mail spread, and electronic billing and even open-source software. Once you insist that those you work with use a method that works, the circles of adoption will get wider.

What's the best way to tell people about the Modern Meeting?

This manifesto was specifically designed to change people's minds. Far greater impact is often achieved through a gift than through just a conversation. So I hope you'll buy and hand copies to everyone in your organization.

More questions?

Share your stories and questions at: ModernMeetingStandard.com.

Acknowledgments

Thanks to Seth Godin and Ishita Gupta for showing me the way. And to the Domino Project team for their amazing work in helping bring my ideas to life.

Special thanks to J. Edward Russo and Paul J.H. Schoemaker who's book, Winning Decisions inspired much of my thinking behind effective decision making.

To Marios Damianides, David Kirschner, Barry Sears, Stanley Chu, Blesson Samuel, Sean Aitken, Harris Kern—mentors along the way.

Shakir Teal, Michael Zumchak, Ashwin Corattiyil, Jonathan Brown, and Daniel Ingala, whom I've always wanted an excuse to shout out.

To April Morley, Kieran Sullivan, Jaimie Joseph, Samantha Nicholson, Jocelyn Chu, Marsh Ahmal, Samuel Slater, Kristopher Deschere, Ronald Davis, Mark Levitt, Cressida Suttles, Joseph Kelleher, Molly Smith, Curtis Williams, Michael Friedman, Joe Kelleher, Zack Serrano, Alex Lasalle—colleagues and friends.

Thanks to Cameron Crowe for the inspiration.

Mom and Dad, of course.

And to everyone whose horrible meetings I've ever had to suffer through, I thank you the most.

About The Domino Project

Books worth buying are books worth sharing. We hope you'll find someone to give this copy to. You can find more about what we're up to at www.thedominoproject.com.

Here are three ways you can spread the ideas in this manifesto:

1. Hold a discussion group in your office. Get people to read the book and come in and argue about it. How open is your company to innovation and failure? What will you do if your competitors get better at it than you are?

2. Give away copies. Lots of them. It turns out that when everyone in a group reads the same thing, conversations go differently.

3. Write the names of some of your peers on the inside back cover of this book (or scrawl them on a Post-it on your Kindle). As each person reads the book, have them scratch off their name and add someone else's.

Tweet your thoughts: #meetDomino

We hope you'll share.

About the Cover

We have a rule at The Domino Project: We don't put words on the covers of our books.

So why are there words on this one?

For two reasons:

A. We know that the modern meeting standard won't catch on unless you share this book with people who might not pick it up on their own. The cover of this book is designed to make it easy for someone to share the idea, and for a person to dive right in.

    and

B. The rules surrounding meetings in your organization are broken. They need to be broken. We figured we'd get you started by breaking one of our rules as well.

Have fun, and more important, go get something done. It matters.